WELCOME
TO YOUR
LIFE CHANGING
MOVEMENT

*Enjoy your tool and LEAD your life
to reach success!*

I'm here to assist you in this exciting journey you're starting. I was designed specially to help you transform dreams to goals and to reality, to help you keep consistency, to overcome procrastination and failure.

You'll see that even some of the most successful people, at a point, were having just a goal and were struggling to make a move towards their goals.

I'm designed to give you clarity on WHAT you want, on the WHY behind your goals and to keep you stubborn on HOW you'll make it a reality.

I'm your accountable friend!

I'm a straight forward journal designed to help you:
- stay focused on what is important to you
- organise your thoughts
- plan the necessary steps
- keep yourself accountable for your progress
- remind yourself to celebrate the progress you make along the way.

Writing down your goals will bring clarity and increased focus. You'll gain confidence that your goals are reachable and find the courage to take small steps towards achieving them.

WHAT you want – write down a clear and very specific goal, use as many details as possible and make it **SMART**.

<u>S</u>pecific: well defined, clear, and unambiguous.

<u>M</u>easurable: with specific criteria that measure your progress toward the accomplishment of the goal.

<u>A</u>chievable: attainable and not impossible to achieve. Setting goals, you can reasonably accomplish within a certain time frame.

<u>R</u>ealistic: within reach, realistic, and relevant to your life. When setting goals for yourself, consider whether they are relevant.

<u>T</u>ime-bound: with a clearly defined timeline, including a starting date and a target date. An end-date can help provide motivation and help you prioritize.

Close our eyes for a moment and imagine your goal is already reached. How does it feel in your heart, mind and body? Remember that feeling!

WHY you want it – take the 7 levels deep exercise to expose why this goal is important to you. Take your time to reveal your deepest motivation and use it as a fuel for your action plan.

Ask yourself: Why is this goal important to me?

> Because ... *your first answer*

Then ask yourself: Why is ... *first answer*... important to me?

> Because ... *your second answer*

Then ask yourself: Why is ... *second answer*... important to me?

> Because ... *your third answer*

Continue doing this until you reach your seventh answer.

It will be your deepest motivation!

For additional guidance on this exercise please check the detailed video by scanning:

HOW to reach it –break the goal into small, easy steps to get you from where you are now to where you want to be.

Break it in as many steps you want or need so it will be easy to accomplish. Throw away the excuses and why it won't work and focus on What You Can Do to move forward. Obsessively ask yourself "What can I do?", "What is the next step?", "What is in my control to change?" and focus on what can go right.

For additional guidance on this exercise please check the detailed video by scanning...

Take the very first step and focus on it until you've accomplished it. Then, with a little more confidence, take the next one and so on, until you have reached your goal.

Celebrate every small step achieved!!!
Make use of the motivational quotes and videos to keep the momentum and the enthusiasm going on "rainy days". Being consistent in journaling keeps you moving closer and closer to your dreams.

Enjoy the journey and be consistent to your goals!

What!?

Why?

How?

DAY   M T W Th F S Su   DATE: /   /

Focus list:

1- ____

____

2- ____

____

3- ____

____

Other things to consider:

____

____

____

____

____

____

Notes:

____

____

____

____

____

DAY M T W Th F S Su   DATE: /   /

Focus list:

1-

2-

3-

Other things to consider:

Notes:

20 minutes of doing something is more valued than 20 hours of thinking about doing something

DAY   M T W Th F S Su   DATE: /   /

Focus list:

1-

2-

3-

Other things to consider:

Notes:

DAY M T W Th F S Su   DATE: /   /

Focus list:

1-

2-

3-

Other things to consider:

Notes:

DAY   M T W Th F S Su   DATE: /   /

Focus list:

1-

2-

3-

Other things to consider:

Notes:

DAY   M T W Th F S Su   DATE: /   /

Focus list:

1-
____

2-
____

3-
____

____

Other things to consider:

____
____
____
____
____

Notes:

____
____
____
____
____

DAY M T W Th F S Su   DATE: /   /

Last step overview

List the things that went well:

____

____

____

____

____

____

Hi 5 to yourself!

What action did you take that went well:

____

____

____

____

____

____

Do more of this!

What action should be adjusted or abandoned:

____

____

____

____

____

____

DAY M T W Th F S Su   DATE: /   /

Next step

List the things that you want for next step, include due dates:

____

____

____

____

____

____

What actions you can & should take:

____

____

____

____

____

Notes &/ NOT to do list:

____

____

____

____

____

____

Enjoy the process!

DAY M T W Th F S Su   DATE: /   /

Focus list:

1-
____

____

2-
____

____

3-
____

____

Other things to consider:

____

____

____

____

____

____

Notes:

____

____

____

____

____

____

DAY M T W Th F S Su   DATE: /   /

Focus list:

1-

2-

3-

Other things to consider:

Notes:

DAY   M T W Th F S Su   DATE: /   /

Focus list:

1-

2-

3-

Other things to consider:

Notes:

DAY M T W Th F S Su   DATE: /   /

Focus list:

1-

2-

3-

Other things to consider:

Notes:

DAY   M T W Th F S Su   DATE: /   /

Focus list:

1- _______________________________________

2- _______________________________________

3- _______________________________________

Other things to consider:

____

____

____

____

____

Notes:

____

____

____

____

____

DAY M T W Th F S Su   DATE: /   /

Focus list:

1-

2-

3-

Other things to consider:

Notes:

DAY M T W Th F S Su   DATE: /   /

Last step overview

List the things that went well:

____

____

____

____

____

____

Hi 5 to yourself!

What action did you take that went well:

____

____

____

____

____

____

Do more of this!

What action should be adjusted or abandoned:

____

____

____

____

____

____

DAY   M T W Th F S Su   DATE: /   /

Next step

List the things that you want for next step, include due dates:

____

____

____

____

____

____

What actions you can & should take:

____

____

____

____

____

Notes &/ NOT to do list:

____

____

____

____

____

Enjoy the process!

DAY M T W Th F S Su   DATE: /   /

Focus list:

1-

2-

3-

Other things to consider:

Notes:

DAY M T W Th F S Su   DATE: /   /

Focus list:

1-
____

2-
____

3-
____

____

Other things to consider:

____
____
____
____
____
____

Notes:

____
____
____
____
____
____

DAY M T W Th F S Su   DATE: /   /

Focus list:

1- ____

2- ____

3- ____

____

Other things to consider:

____

____

____

____

____

____

Notes:

____

____

____

____

____

____

DAY M T W Th F S Su   DATE: /   /

Focus list:

1-

2-

3-

Other things to consider:

Notes:

You never know how strong you are until being strong is the only choice you have –
Bob Marley

DAY   M T W Th F S Su   DATE: /   /

Focus list:

1- ____

2- ____

3- ____

____

Other things to consider:

____
____
____
____
____
____

Notes:

____
____
____
____
____

DAY   M T W Th F S Su   DATE: /   /

Focus list:

1-

2-

3-

Other things to consider:

Notes:

DAY   M T W Th F S Su   DATE: /   /

Last step overview

List the things that went well:

____

____

____

____

____

____

What action did you take that went well:

____

____

____

____

____

What action should be adjusted or abandoned:

____

____

____

____

____

DAY M T W Th F S Su   DATE: /   /

Next step

List the things that you want for next step, include due dates:

____

____

____

____

____

____

What actions you can & should take:

____

____

____

____

____

Notes &/ NOT to do list:

____

____

____

____

____

____

Enjoy the process!

The secret of change is to focus all of your energy, not on fighting the old, but on building the new — Socrates

DAY M T W Th F S Su   DATE: /   /

Focus list:

1- ______________________________

____

2- ______________________________

____

3- ______________________________

____

____

Other things to consider:

____

____

____

____

____

____

Notes:

____

____

____

____

____

DAY M T W Th F S Su   DATE: /   /

Focus list:

1- ____

2- ____

3- ____

____

Other things to consider:

____

____

____

____

____

____

Notes:

____

____

____

____

____

____

DAY M T W Th F S Su   DATE: /   /

Focus list:

1-

2-

3-

Other things to consider:

Notes:

DAY   M T W Th F S Su   DATE: /   /

Focus list:

1-

2-

3-

Other things to consider:

Notes:

DAY M T W Th F S Su   DATE: /   /

Focus list:

1-

2-

3-

Other things to consider:

Notes:

DAY M T W Th F S Su   DATE: /   /

Focus list:

1-

2-

3-

Other things to consider:

Notes:

DAY M T W Th F S Su   DATE: /   /

Last step overview

List the things that went well:

____

____

____

____

____

____

Hi 5 to yourself!

What action did you take that went well:

____

____

____

____

____

____

Do more of this!

What action should be adjusted or abandoned:

____

____

____

____

____

____

DAY   M T W Th F S Su   DATE: /   /

Next step

List the things that you want for next step, include due dates:

____

____

____

____

____

____

What actions you can & should take:

____

____

____

____

____

Notes &/ NOT to do list:

____

____

____

____

____

Enjoy the process!

DAY M T W Th F S Su   DATE: /   /

Focus list:

1-

2-

3-

Other things to consider:

Notes:

DAY M T W Th F S Su   DATE: /   /

Focus list:

1-

2-

3-

Other things to consider:

Notes:

DAY M T W Th F S Su   DATE: /   /

Focus list:

1- ____

2- ____

3- ____

____

Other things to consider:

____
____
____
____
____

Notes:

____
____
____
____
____

DAY   M T W Th F S Su   DATE: /   /

Focus list:

1-

2-

3-

Other things to consider:

Notes:

DAY   M T W Th F S Su   DATE: /   /

Focus list:

1-

2-

3-

Other things to consider:

Notes:

DAY M T W Th F S Su   DATE: /   /

Focus list:

1- ____

2- ____

3- ____

____

Other things to consider:

____
____
____
____
____
____

Notes:

____
____
____
____
____

When life give you a hundred reasons to break down and cry, show life that you have a million reasons to smile and to be thankful for. Stay strong!

DAY M T W Th F S Su   DATE: /   /

Last step overview

List the things that went well:

____

____

____

____

____

____

Hi 5 to yourself!

What action did you take that went well:

____

____

____

____

____

____

Do more of this!

What action should be adjusted or abandoned:

____

____

____

____

____

____

DAY M T W Th F S Su   DATE: /   /

Next step

List the things that you want for next step, include due dates:

____

____

____

____

____

____

What actions you can & should take:

____

____

____

____

____

____

Notes &/ NOT to do list:

____

____

____

____

____

Enjoy the process!

DAY   M T W Th F S Su   DATE: /   /

Focus list:

1-
____

2-
____

3-
____

____

Other things to consider:

____
____
____
____
____
____

Notes:

____
____
____
____
____
____

DAY M T W Th F S Su   DATE: /   /

Focus list:

1-

2-

3-

Other things to consider:

Notes:

DAY M T W Th F S Su   DATE: /   /

Focus list:

1-

2-

3-

Other things to consider:

Notes:

DAY M T W Th F S Su   DATE: /   /

Focus list:

1-

2-

3-

Other things to consider:

Notes:

DAY M T W Th F S Su   DATE: /   /

Focus list:

1-
____

2-
____

3-
____

____

Other things to consider:

____
____
____
____
____

Notes:

____
____
____
____
____

DAY M T W Th F S Su   DATE: /   /

Focus list:

1-

2-

3-

Other things to consider:

Notes:

DAY M T W Th F S Su   DATE: /   /

Last step overview

List the things that went well:

____

____

____

____

____

____

Hi 5 to yourself!

What action did you take that went well:

____

____

____

____

____

____

Do more of this!

What action should be adjusted or abandoned:

____

____

____

____

____

____

DAY   M T W Th F S Su   DATE: /   /

Next step

List the things that you want for next step, include due dates:

____

____

____

____

____

____

What actions you can & should take:

____

____

____

____

____

____

Notes &/ NOT to do list:

____

____

____

____

____

____

Enjoy the process!

DAY   M T W Th F S Su   DATE: /   /

Focus list:

1- ____

2- ____

3- ____

____

Other things to consider:

____
____
____
____
____

Notes:

____
____
____
____
____

DAY M T W Th F S Su   DATE: /   /

Focus list:

1-

2-

3-

Other things to consider:

Notes:

DAY   M T W Th F S Su   DATE: /   /

Focus list:

1-
____

2-
____

3-
____

____

Other things to consider:

____

____

____

____

____

Notes:

____

____

____

____

____

DAY M T W Th F S Su   DATE: /   /

Focus list:

1-

2-

3-

Other things to consider:

Notes:

DAY   M T W Th F S Su   DATE: /   /

Focus list:

1-

2-

3-

Other things to consider:

Notes:

DAY M T W Th F S Su   DATE: /   /

Focus list:

1-

2-

3-

Other things to consider:

Notes:

DAY M T W Th F S Su   DATE: /   /

Last step overview

List the things that went well:

____

____

____

____

____

____

Hi 5 to yourself!

What action did you take that went well:

____

____

____

____

____

____

Do more of this!

What action should be adjusted or abandoned:

____

____

____

____

____

DAY   M T W Th F S Su   DATE: /   /

Next step

List the things that you want for next step, include due dates:

____

____

____

____

____

____

What actions you can & should take:

____

____

____

____

____

____

Notes &/ NOT to do list:

____

____

____

____

____

____

Enjoy the process!

DAY M T W Th F S Su   DATE: /   /

Focus list:

1-

2-

3-

Other things to consider:

Notes:

DAY   M T W Th F S Su   DATE: /   /

Focus list:

1-

2-

3-

Other things to consider:

Notes:

DAY M T W Th F S Su   DATE: /   /

Focus list:

1-
____

2-
____

3-
____

Other things to consider:

____
____
____
____
____

Notes:

____
____
____
____
____

DAY   M T W Th F S Su   DATE: /   /

Focus list:

1-

2-

3-

Other things to consider:

Notes:

DAY M T W Th F S Su   DATE: /   /

Focus list:

1-

2-

3-

Other things to consider:

Notes:

DAY   M T W Th F S Su   DATE: /   /

Focus list:

1-

2-

3-

Other things to consider:

Notes:

DAY   M T W Th F S Su   DATE: /   /

Last step overview

List the things that went well:

____

____

____

____

____

____

Hi 5 to yourself !

What action did you take that went well:

____

____

____

____

____

Do more of this!

What action should be adjusted or abandoned:

____

____

____

____

____

DAY M T W Th F S Su   DATE: /   /

Next step

List the things that you want for next step, include due dates:

____

____

____

____

____

____

What actions you can & should take:

____

____

____

____

____

____

Notes &/ NOT to do list:

____

____

____

____

____

____

Enjoy the process!

DAY   M T W Th F S Su   DATE: /   /

Focus list:

1-

2-

3-

Other things to consider:

Notes:

DAY   M T W Th F S Su   DATE: /   /

Focus list:

1-

2-

3-

Other things to consider:

Notes:

DAY   M T W Th F S Su   DATE: /   /

Focus list:

1-

2-

3-

Other things to consider:

Notes:

DAY   M T W Th F S Su   DATE: /   /

Focus list:

1-

2-

3-

Other things to consider:

Notes:

DAY M T W Th F S Su   DATE: /   /

Focus list:

1-

2-

3-

Other things to consider:

Notes:

DAY   M T W Th F S Su   DATE: /   /

Focus list:

1-
____

2-
____

3-
____

____

Other things to consider:

____
____
____
____
____
____

Notes:

____
____
____
____
____
____

Mirror mirror on the wall. I'll always get up after I fall and whether I run, walk or crawl, I'll set my goals and achieve them all. - Brie Edison

DAY   M T W Th F S Su   DATE: /   /

Last step overview

List the things that went well:

____

____

____

____

____

____

Hi 5 to yourself!

What action did you take that went well:

____

____

____

____

____

____

Do more of this!

What action should be adjusted or abandoned:

____

____

____

____

____

DAY   M T W Th F S Su   DATE: /   /

Next step

List the things that you want for next step, include due dates:

____

____

____

____

____

What actions you can & should take:

____

____

____

____

____

Notes &/ NOT to do list:

____

____

____

____

____

Enjoy the process!

DAY   M T W Th F S Su   DATE: /   /

Focus list:

1-

2-

3-

Other things to consider:

Notes:

DAY M T W Th F S Su   DATE: /   /

Focus list:

1-

2-

3-

Other things to consider:

Notes:

Too many people think the grass is greener somewhere else, but the glass is green where you water it. Remember that!

DAY M T W Th F S Su   DATE: /   /

Focus list:

1-
____

2-
____

3-
____

____

Other things to consider:

____

____

____

____

____

____

Notes:

____

____

____

____

____

DAY   M T W Th F S Su   DATE: /   /

Focus list:

1-

2-

3-

Other things to consider:

Notes:

DAY M T W Th F S Su   DATE: /   /

Focus list:

1-

2-

3-

Other things to consider:

Notes:

DAY   M T W Th F S Su   DATE: /   /

Focus list:

1-

2-

3-

Other things to consider:

Notes:

DAY M T W Th F S Su   DATE: /   /

Last step overview

List the things that went well:

____

____

____

____

____

____

Hi 5 to yourself!

What action did you take that went well:

____

____

____

____

____

____

Do more of this!

What action should be adjusted or abandoned:

____

____

____

____

____

____

DAY M T W Th F S Su   DATE: /   /

Next step

List the things that you want for next step, include due dates:

____

____

____

____

____

What actions you can & should take:

____

____

____

____

____

Notes &/ NOT to do list:

____

____

____

____

____

If someone tells you "you can't" they're showing you their limits. Not yours!

DAY M T W Th F S Su   DATE: /   /

Focus list:

1-
____

____

2-
____

____

3-
____

____

Other things to consider:

____

____

____

____

____

Notes:

____

____

____

____

____

DAY   M T W Th F S Su   DATE: /   /

Focus list:

1-

2-

3-

Other things to consider:

Notes:

Money is nothing more than a reflection of your creativity, your capacity to focus, and your ability to add value and receive back. - Anthony Robbins

DAY   M T W Th F S Su   DATE: /   /

Focus list:

1-

2-

3-

Other things to consider:

Notes:

DAY M T W Th F S Su   DATE: /   /

Focus list:

1-
____

2-
____

3-
____

____

Other things to consider:

____
____
____
____
____
____

Notes:

____
____
____
____
____
____

DAY   M T W Th F S Su   DATE: /   /

Focus list:

1-
____

____

2-
____

3-
____

____

Other things to consider:

____

____

____

____

____

____

Notes:

____

____

____

____

____

DAY M T W Th F S Su   DATE: /   /

Focus list:

1-

2-

3-

Other things to consider:

Notes:

DAY   M T W Th F S Su   DATE: /   /

Last step overview

List the things that went well:

____

____

____

____

____

____

Hi 5 to yourself !

What action did you take that went well:

____

____

____

____

____

____

Do more of this!

What action should be adjusted or abandoned:

____

____

____

____

____

____

DAY M T W Th F S Su   DATE: /   /

Next step

List the things that you want for next step, include due dates:

____

____

____

____

____

What actions you can & should take:

____

____

____

____

____

Notes &/ NOT to do list:

____

____

____

____

____

Enjoy the process!

DAY   M T W Th F S Su   DATE: /   /

Focus list:

1- ____

2- ____

3- ____

____

Other things to consider:

____

____

____

____

____

____

Notes:

____

____

____

____

____

DAY   M T W Th F S Su   DATE: /   /

Focus list:

1-
____

2-
____

3-
____

____

Other things to consider:

____
____
____
____
____
____

Notes:

____
____
____
____
____
____

DAY M T W Th F S Su   DATE: /   /

Focus list:

1-

2-

3-

Other things to consider:

Notes:

DAY M T W Th F S Su   DATE: /   /

Focus list:

1-

2-

3-

Other things to consider:

Notes:

DAY M T W Th F S Su   DATE: /   /

Focus list:

1- ____

2- ____

3- ____

Other things to consider:

____

____

____

____

____

Notes:

____

____

____

____

____

DAY   M T W Th F S Su   DATE: /   /

Focus list:

1-
____

2-
____

3-
____

____

Other things to consider:

____
____
____
____
____
____

Notes:

____
____
____
____
____
____

DAY   M T W Th F S Su   DATE: /   /

Last step overview

List the things that went well:

____

____

____

____

____

____

Hi 5 to yourself !

What action did you take that went well:

____

____

____

____

____

____

Do more of this!

What action should be adjusted or abandoned:

____

____

____

____

____

DAY   M T W Th F S Su   DATE: /   /

Next step

List the things that you want for next step, include due dates:

____

____

____

____

____

____

What actions you can & should take:

____

____

____

____

____

Notes &/ NOT to do list:

____

____

____

____

____

Enjoy the process!

DAY   M T W Th F S Su   DATE: /   /

Focus list:

1-
____

____

2-
____

____

3-
____

____

Other things to consider:

____

____

____

____

____

____

Notes:

____

____

____

____

____

____

DAY   M T W Th F S Su   DATE: /   /

Focus list:

1-
____

2-
____

3-
____

____

Other things to consider:

____
____
____
____
____
____

Notes:

____
____
____
____
____
____

DAY M T W Th F S Su   DATE: /   /

Focus list:

1- ____

2- ____

3- ____

Other things to consider:

____

____

____

____

____

Notes:

____

____

____

____

DAY   M T W Th F S Su   DATE: /   /

Focus list:

1-
____

2-
____

3-
____

____

Other things to consider:

____
____
____
____
____
____

Notes:

____
____
____
____
____
____

DAY   M T W Th F S Su   DATE: /   /

Focus list:

1-

2-

3-

Other things to consider:

Notes:

DAY   M T W Th F S Su   DATE: /   /

Focus list:

1-
____

____

2-
____

____

3-
____

____

Other things to consider:

____

____

____

____

____

____

Notes:

____

____

____

____

____

____

Look back at where you came from and let yourself feel proud about your progress.
You are killing it!

DAY   M T W Th F S Su   DATE: /   /

Last step overview

List the things that went well:

____

____

____

____

____

____

Hi 5 to yourself !

What action did you take that went well:

____

____

____

____

____

Do more of this!

What action should be adjusted or abandoned:

____

____

____

____

____

____

DAY   M T W Th F S Su   DATE: /   /

Next step

List the things that you want for next step, include due dates:

____

____

____

____

____

____

What actions you can & should take:

____

____

____

____

____

Notes &/ NOT to do list:

____

____

____

____

____

DAY M T W Th F S Su   DATE: /   /

Focus list:

1-

2-

3-

Other things to consider:

Notes:

DAY M T W Th F S Su   DATE: /   /

Focus list:

1-
____

2-
____

3-
____

Other things to consider:

____
____
____
____
____
____

Notes:

____
____
____
____
____

DAY M T W Th F S Su   DATE: /   /

Focus list:

1-
____

____

2-
____

____

3-
____

____

Other things to consider:

____

____

____

____

____

____

Notes:

____

____

____

____

____

DAY M T W Th F S Su   DATE: /   /

Focus list:

1-

2-

3-

Other things to consider:

Notes:

DAY   M T W Th F S Su   DATE: /   /

Focus list:

1-

2-

3-

Other things to consider:

Notes:

DAY M T W Th F S Su   DATE: /   /

Focus list:

1-
____

2-
____

3-
____

Other things to consider:

____
____
____
____
____
____

Notes:

____
____
____
____
____
____

DAY   M T W Th F S Su   DATE: /   /

Last step overview

List the things that went well:

____

____

____

____

____

____

Hi 5 to yourself!

What action did you take that went well:

____

____

____

____

____

Do more of this!

What action should be adjusted or abandoned:

____

____

____

____

____

DAY   M T W Th F S Su   DATE: /   /

Next step

List the things that you want for next step, include due dates:

____

____

____

____

____

What actions you can & should take:

____

____

____

____

____

Notes &/ NOT to do list:

____

____

____

____

____

Enjoy the process!

Always believe in yourself

DAY M T W Th F S Su   DATE: /   /

Focus list:

1- ____

2- ____

3- ____

Other things to consider:

____

____

____

____

____

Notes:

____

____

____

____

____

DAY M T W Th F S Su   DATE: /   /

Focus list:

1-

2-

3-

Other things to consider:

Notes:

Failure is a part of life. If you don't fail, you don't learn. If you don't learn, you'll never change

DAY M T W Th F S Su   DATE: /   /

Focus list:

1-

____

2-

____

3-

____

____

Other things to consider:

____

____

____

____

____

Notes:

____

____

____

____

____

DAY M T W Th F S Su   DATE: /   /

Focus list:

1-

2-

3-

Other things to consider:

Notes:

DAY   M T W Th F S Su   DATE: /   /

Focus list:

1-
____

2-
____

3-
____

____

Other things to consider:

____
____
____
____
____

Notes:

____
____
____
____
____

DAY   M T W Th F S Su   DATE: /   /

Focus list:

1-

2-

3-

Other things to consider:

Notes:

DAY   M T W Th F S Su   DATE: /   /

Last step overview

List the things that went well:

____

____

____

____

____

____

Hi 5 to yourself!

What action did you take that went well:

____

____

____

____

____

____

Do more of this!

What action should be adjusted or abandoned:

____

____

____

____

____

____

DAY M T W Th F S Su   DATE: /   /

Next step

List the things that you want for next step, include due dates:

____

____

____

____

____

____

What actions you can & should take:

____

____

____

____

____

____

Notes &/ NOT to do list:

____

____

____

____

____

____

Enjoy the process!

DAY   M T W Th F S Su   DATE: /   /

Focus list:

1-

2-

3-

Other things to consider:

Notes:

DAY M T W Th F S Su   DATE: /   /

Focus list:

1-

2-

3-

Other things to consider:

Notes:

DAY M T W Th F S Su   DATE: /   /

Focus list:

1-
____

2-
____

3-
____

____

Other things to consider:

____
____
____
____
____
____

Notes:

____
____
____
____
____
____

DAY M T W Th F S Su   DATE: /   /

Focus list:

1-

2-

3-

Other things to consider:

Notes:

DAY   M T W Th F S Su   DATE: /   /

Focus list:

1-

2-

3-

Other things to consider:

Notes:

DAY   M T W Th F S Su   DATE: /   /

Focus list:

1-

2-

3-

Other things to consider:

Notes:

DAY   M T W Th F S Su   DATE: /   /

Last step overview

List the things that went well:

____

____

____

____

____

____

What action did you take that went well:

____

____

____

____

____

What action should be adjusted or abandoned:

____

____

____

____

____

DAY M T W Th F S Su   DATE: /   /

Next step

List the things that you want for next step, include due dates:

____

____

____

____

____

____

What actions you can & should take:

____

____

____

____

____

____

Notes &/ NOT to do list:

____

____

____

____

____

Enjoy the process!

Congratulations

Made in the USA
Columbia, SC
08 June 2024